Look at That Building!

A First Book of Structures

Scot Ritchie

W
FRANKLIN WATTS
LONDON•SYDNEY

Dedicated to my dad, Ross Ritchie,
one of Canada's great architects – S.R.

Franklin Watts

First published in Great Britain in 2017 by
The Watts Publishing Group

Text and illustrations © 2011 Scot Ritchie

Published by permission of Kids Can Press Ltd.,
Toronto, Ontario, Canada.

www.kidscanpress.com

Edited by Samantha Swenson
Designed by Julia Naimska

ISBN 978 1 4451 5371 1

Manufactured in Malaysia in 11/2016 by
Tien Wah Press (Pte.) Ltd.

Franklin Watts
An imprint of Hachette Children's Group
Part of The Watts Publishing Group
Carmelite House
50 Victoria Embankment
London EC4Y 0DZ

An Hachette UK company
www.hachette.co.uk

www.franklinwatts.co.uk

Contents

Buildings All Around Us

You've probably noticed that your home has floors, walls and windows. But did you know it might have foundations, a frame and beams, too? Let's go for a walk with our five friends to find out how buildings are put together.

Yulee Martin Max Nick Pedro Sally Ollie

A building is a structure: something that is made of different parts. Buildings are all around us and have lots of different uses.

Home Plans

Sally's dad has built her a tree house. Her friends have come over to see it. What a great little building! Everybody is having fun except Max. He can't climb up to join them.

People build everywhere: on water, on top of cliffs, in trees and even underground!

Firm Foundations

Yulee thinks that such a deep hole must have taken a lot of digging. Martin is watching the construction workers pour concrete. The foundations are going to be very strong.

Foundations are the lowest part of a building. It keeps the rest of the building stable by anchoring it securely in the ground.

The taller a building is, the deeper and larger its foundations have to be. Some skyscrapers' foundations go four storeys under the ground!

A Place to Stand

Next stop: the library! Pedro is making sure the floor is solid enough to hold all of these books.

A floor is the surface we stand on in a building. Floors are made of very durable materials so that they last a long time.

Floors can be made from many different materials, including wood, stone and concrete.

Look Up!

As they leave the library, Nick notices the beams above his head. They are wide and very long. How many beams can you see?

A beam is usually a long, thick piece of wood, stone or metal. It is rigid so that it can support floors, ceilings and other building parts. You can't always see the beams, but most structures have them.

The first beams were probably made from tree trunks.

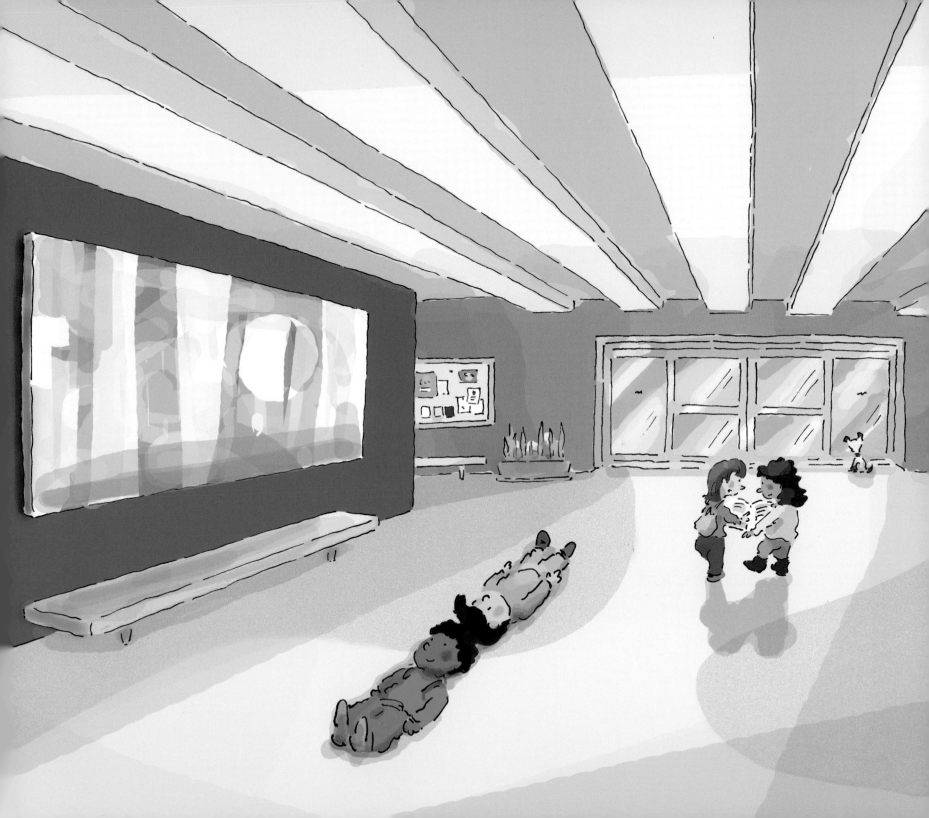

Nature's Buildings

Some animals build their own homes. Sadly, Max can't build his own kennel! Yulee decides they will just have to do a great job for him.

To make their nests, wasps chew tiny bits of wood into a pulp. Then they spit out the pulp and pat it into place with their feet. When it hardens, they have a waterproof home!

Most birds make nests, too. They use twigs, leaves and sometimes even spiders' webs. They weave the materials together to make a place to raise their young. What other animal homes can you see?

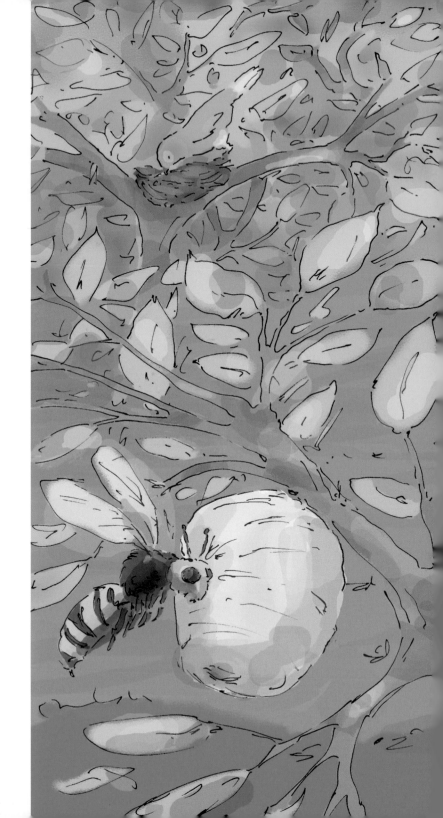

Up the Wall

Yulee looks in a window at her school. She read at the library that walls do more than just hold up the blackboard.

Walls do many important things. They divide a building into rooms and keep the outside … outside. They also help keep the roof up.

Old castle walls are made of stone. They can be up to 6 metres thick!

Frame It!

Pedro looks up at the skyscrapers. He can see right through one of them because it is still being built. Pedro is looking at the building's frame.

Frames can be made of wood, steel or concrete. A frame gives the structure shape and support. Other parts, such as beams and walls, are built on top of the frame.

A frame is a bit like your skeleton. Without it, there would be nothing holding you up from the inside!

Super Shapes

Sally has been to the town hall before. She remembers the dome. Look how big it is!

Three shapes are used in a lot of buildings because they are so strong.

An **arch** is a structure that is curved at the top. The arch shape helps spread weight evenly.

A **dome** is also curved at the top and helps spread the weight of a structure. It can cover a large space with few supports.

A **triangle** is the strongest shape. Lots of weight can be added to a triangle and its shape won't change.

Cool Columns

The columns of this bus shelter remind Yulee of trees. They remind Nick of the columns on his porch at home.

Columns are used to hold up parts of a structure, such as the roof. Because they support so much weight, they have to be made of sturdy materials.

Columns are like beams, except one is vertical and the other is horizontal. They both provide support.

Indoor and Outdoor

Sally loves to look through the windows in the big door at the fire station. The door lets light in and lets fire engines out – in a hurry!

Most buildings have doors and windows. Doors allow people (and pets) to come and go. Windows allow light (or sometimes a nice breeze) to come in.

**Not all windows and doors are in walls.
Sometimes they are in the roof or
even in the floor!**

24

A Roof Over Our Heads

It's raining – time to find somewhere dry. Martin suggests they go back to the tree house. Pedro is glad they will have a roof protecting them.

A roof is the top covering of a building. It shelters the building from the weather.

Some roofs have grass growing on them. They are called green roofs because they help the environment.

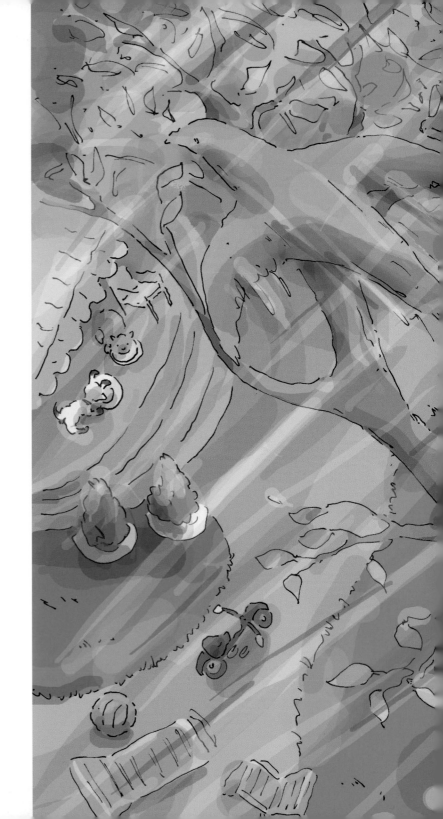

Back at the Tree House

The gang is happy to be back at the cosy tree house. Max is still downstairs, keeping dry on the porch. Soon he will have a cosy house of his very own!

Make a Mini Kennel

Here's a plan for making a mini kennel. You'll need: marshmallows, craft sticks, craft paper, scissors, glue and tape.

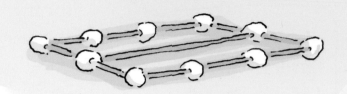

Step 1: Build a frame for the floor using marshmallows and craft sticks.

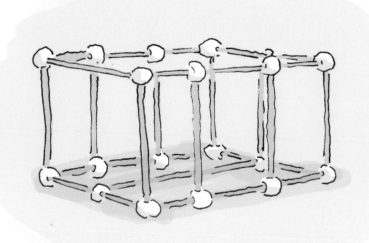

Step 2: Add the frame for the walls.

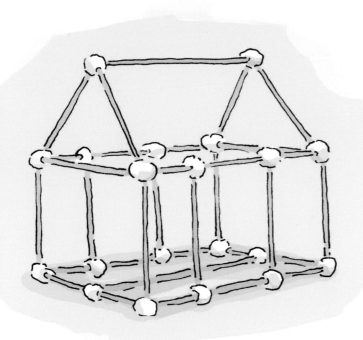

Step 3: Add a peak for the roof.

Step 4: Ask an adult to cut the paper to fit the roof and walls.

Step 5: Glue and tape the paper to the frame.

Index